HOOP!
DON'T SHOOT!

My Concealed Weapon is Love

ANGIENETTE DIXON

PAGE PUBLISHING, INC.
Conneaut Lake, PA

First originally published by Page Publishing 2021

ISBN 978-1-6624-6427-0 (pbk)
ISBN 978-1-6624-6428-7 (digital)

Printed in the United States of America

I would like to thank God, the Hoop Don't Shoot board, and my mom.

Hoop! Don't Shoot! is a story of how God can bring young, old, poor, rich, Black, White, Christian, and secular together, to see that His will is done. It is a story of how love and compassion changes people. Yes, we have had a few setbacks, but our success has outweighed each setback. God is love.

CHAPTER 1
PUT YOUR GUNS DOWN

Pop! Pop! Pop!

Is that gunshots? I thought.

"That's gunshots!" I yelled to my mama. "I'm not running! I'm standing right here!"

Me and my mama were standing right in the middle of the court where bullets were flying. We were just standing there. We didn't duck, get on the ground, or run. We just stood there.

There was so much commotion, and all of a sudden, two young men came running toward us and got right behind me and Mama while the sound of bullets being fired continued. They had sweat pouring out, and they were panting with fast, shallow breaths. The fear in their face told it all, but I asked anyway, "Is somebody shooting at y'all?" The nods confirmed what I thought.

No one was shot that day, and I knew there was no other explanation except for the hand of God protecting us. I found out that the Northside was shooting at the Southside young man that day. This would be an ongoing theme.

Sometimes, it was the Southside shooting at the Northside. Other times, it was the Northside shooting at the Southside. Someone always retaliating. I found out quickly that this wouldn't be the last time this story played out in the streets of Danville, Virginia, with the young men and women that God had called me, Angienette

Dixon, to assist. Little did I know, that God was planting the seeds of Hoop Don't Shoot in me.

> But you are a chosen people, a royal priesthood, a holy nation, God's special possession, *that you may declare the praises of him who called you out of darkness into his wonderful light.* Once you were not a people, but now you are the people of God; once you had not received mercy, but now you have received mercy. (1 Peter 2:9–10)

Man, I ain't no snitch. Those were the words that echoed during the neighborhood. Gang violence and all its issues were running rampant through the city. Southside versus Northside was like a bad divorce in the tabloids. The city was on fire.

Many residents were feeling the pressure of the violence in the city. People were frightened to go outside. The word *Danville* had become synonymous with gun violence. Many people in the community were having workshops, marches, and rallies to make a positive statement in the community. I wanted to make a difference in my community. I understood the code and the often-misplaced loyalty. I knew I had to do something to make a difference.

Many of these kids were caught in the cross fire of life. Their lives were not reflections of their promise. Their circumstances were placing limits on their abilities. Their destinies were being railroaded by their zip codes.

I knew I had to do something to change the narrative around these young men. I knew I had a mission. *My purpose was predestined by God. Yes, even in my jail cell, I was chosen.*

There are a lot of very good people in my neighborhood. They strive, as most of us do, to make positive choices for their families and community. They love their families and care about their communities. There are people in my neighborhood that have lived there for years. They are more than neighbors; many of them consider each other to be family. This is not the story you often see in the news. However, I know it to be true.

There are many good things happening in the area. Hoop Don't Shoot happens to be one of positive changes in the area. It is not only transforming the lives of kids, but it touches the lives of so many adults who have involvement in the program. It is hard not to be involved in a God's ordained ministry and not be positively impacted. It is my God's grace and mercy that the program is thriving and causing great impact of city.

Me and Mom

The first flyer ever

CHAPTER 2
CALLED BY HIS PURPOSE

Smack!

"What do you know about that?" I yelled in the middle of dropping my cards on the table.

The cards on the table were a much-needed distraction from the issues that were swarming in my head.

"Girl, you think you know what you are doing, huh?" another inmate shouted.

The dingy walls were my temporary home. A place that I thought I would never see again.

Rubbing my pregnant belly caused me to reflect on my life. How did I end back in this situation?

Not only was I back in prison but I was pregnant and in prison.

"Girl, get your head back in the game," an inmate yelled.

I put on a fake smile. Outwardly, I was just being good old Angie. Inwardly, my spirit was being chipped minute by minute.

Never, never in a million years did I see myself giving birth in prison.

I had been in the Fluvanna Correctional Center for Women for approximately two weeks. I had been transported from my hometown jail. I did not want to give birth to my baby in prison. I had hoped against all odds to at least be able to remain in the correctional facility in Danville, Virginia.

Going up the long and lonely road was a dark time in my life. No, it was not my first time entering those gates.

However, I felt that my life had taken a new direction. Yes, I still indulged in some mess. However, the charges that had been brought against me appeared petty and unwarranted. Simply, I did not belong in my current residence. My heart was troubled. I knew that the children I had birthed and the child growing in my womb deserved better. I knew that a change was going to have to occur. *The change had to start with me.*

My thoughts were interrupted by a knowing presence. I felt something warm dripping down my legs. I did not want to entertain the thoughts. I kept playing cards and talking smack with the ladies. I kept up the charade as long as I could. Eventually the sergeant was called.

However, I knew that the joy of giving birth would be short-lived. Giving birth in prison is far from the fairytale you encounter on the outside.

I finally arrived at the hospital after putting off the sadness that would occur immediately after birth.

Thirty minutes after my arrival, I gave birth to my beautiful baby girl, Zion. It was one of the most beautiful moments in my life and also, one of the most painful moments in my life. The pain during birth was unparallel to the pain I felt after her birth. I knew that my time with her would be very limited. I knew that my heart would feel horrific pain.

I gazed into her eyes. It was literally love at first sight. I smelled her. I held her. I loved her. I knew that she deserved more than I could provide for her in my current circumstances. I vowed to make it up to her and the rest of my children. A knock on the door interrupted my thoughts. I knew the knock signaled a blow to my heart.

"Angie, we need to take the baby," a voice stated.

I gazed around to the time, thirty minutes. Thirty minutes was all the time I had with my baby. This was too cruel. I felt like my heart was being ripped from my body.

I could not believe what was happening in my life. My mind and heart were all lost in a whirlwind of emotions. Each one losing the fight to the reality that waited for me on the other side of the daughter.

Questions and sadness enveloped my mind. What would happen to her? Would she know me? Would she hate me?

I was scared and hurt. I could not let them take my baby away from me.

Bang, Bang. The door rattled with anticipation on the other side of the door. I had to think of something quick. I did the only thing I knew to do at the time, I ran.

I ran to the bathroom. Tears and sweat formed, beading flowing down my face. I knew this was only an unrealistic solution to my problem. But I wanted to seize any amount of time I could would my newborn. Soft voices attempted to ease the turmoil inside of me.

"Angie, please come out and hand her over."

I opened the door. I handed my beautiful baby over to the nurse. The grief that surrounded me was overwhelming.

I was eventually handcuffed and driven back to the prison. The short ride to the prison felt like another sentence.

Knowing that my baby would spend an overnight stay in the hospital alone was gut-wrenching. My mother was coming to pick her up the next day. The fact that she would be with family was a little soothing. The fact that she would be away from me for two years was heartbreaking.

Little did I know the restoration God had in my path. After two years of incarnation, my baby knew me without question.

My life had been riddled with questions. God's restoration would help me heal and assist others in their process.

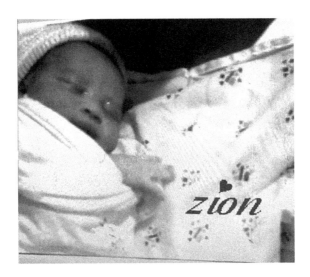

My daughter Zion from the hospital that day to now in college with A's. She is a sophomore at Ferrum College with two part time jobs.

CHAPTER 3

MY IDENTITY

I was raised in the country on a farm. We may not have had a whole lot of materialistic things, but we had love. My daddy provided for us the best he could. We may not always have had all we wanted and may not always have had the best clothes or food, but we survived and were happy. My brothers and sisters and I were raised in church. As a matter of fact, we went two or three nights each week. As a young girl, I loved going to church. I always loved Jesus. He has been my friend all my life. I always had conversations with God. I would look up to the sky and ask God's opinion on a lot of things I didn't understand.

My daddy and mama had five more kids after me, so there were nine of us all together. We were very poor, but I didn't really realize it. We lived in Chatham out in the country. We didn't have much, but we had love.

We had to bring water to the house for drinking because we had no running water in the house. We had no bathroom; we had to go out to an outhouse. We had no heat. We had to cut up lots of firewood and build fires to warm ourselves. It got very cold in there, and it was hard to stay warm.

We moved to Danville, and we were so happy because there we had indoor plumbing with running water in the house for the kitchen and the bathroom. No more going to the outhouse. We were loving it! We were also able to go the local high school. Me and my family liked being in Danville.

Me and some of my siblings from a long time ago

Also a picture of me now changed happy

CHAPTER 4

THE CALLING

Therefore, if anyone is in Christ, he is a new cre-
ation. The old has passed away; behold, the new
has come. (2 Corinthians 5:17)

*Over the years, the pieces of the puzzle of my life started to come together. I
found God to be my deliver, protector, and healer. He is the lover of my soul
and the restorer of my life.* Once you become saved, you want the same joy
and peace you feel to be felt by others around you. I could see that many
of the youth around me were struggling with making good decisions. I
did not want them to fall into the same traps that kept me in bondage.

My calling to minister to these young men came at a funeral.
It was June 5, 2017, and I was staring into the casket of yet another
young man, dead from my hometown. I couldn't stop the tears. They
just kept falling. I was crying emotionally and spiritually.

This wasn't the first funeral of a teenager I had been to. The
funerals just seemed to keep happening, and it was like nobody had

answers for how to stop them. People were walking by looking into the face of youth that should be vibrant with life still ahead of them. Instead, this youth was in a box, being ready to be lowered into the ground. The finality of it all was overwhelming to me!

Then, I heard the Holy Spirit speak to me in my spirit, and He said, *That young man lying in the casket didn't know me. And the young man who shot him doesn't know that I love him and would forgive him.* That hit me so hard.

I knew I had to do something to reach these young men caught up in gangs in the area. Jesus could stop the shootings. Nothing was too hard for Him. They need to hear how much He loves them. If I can get that message to them, things will change.

The gospel changes lives! I couldn't deny that the Lord had spoken that day, and I had to obey the calling. I left that funeral with a very specific, God-given purpose. I didn't know how, but I would follow the Lord's lead.

That very same afternoon, my then fifteen-year-old daughter and I went to the park to shoot hoops. Three young men were already there. We played basketball together, and I could see the light in their eyes. We connected playing basketball. *Lord, this is what you want me to use to fish with—a basketball!*

The vision God had given me was very clear. All in the same day, He had called me. By providing a way for me to build a bridge, to share that He is able to deliver His children, change their lives, and bring them out of bondage.

I started showing up to the basketball court several times a week, and every time I showed up at least five boys would be there. We would play ball. We would connect. *Lord, you are helping me build this bridge using basketball.*

This was happening quickly. They would ask, "Ms. Lady (they hadn't learned my name yet), do you have anything to eat?" I soon realized they were hungry physically.

I said, "Okay, God you want me to feed their bodies and their stomachs."

Some questioned my ability to do this ministry. However, my journey prepared me for this mission.

First picture and tournament, also the start of
how many we had at the beginning.

CHAPTER 5

LOVE HIDES A MULTITUDE OF SINS

God prepared me for this job. I was trained and built for this. When I was fifteen years old, my dad was hauling pulpwood in addition to tobacco farming. It was a serious job; the work was terribly hard and dangerous. One evening at home, we were listening to WKBY radio station from Chatham, Virginia, and a song was playing which I remember until today. "I'm coming up on the rough side of the mountain, and I'm doing my best to make it in." The lyrics were a household song at that time.

Well, while we were listening, the phone rang, and my mother was informed that my dad had been in an accident and was pronounced dead. We were all so heartbroken. My mother even passed out. After regaining consciousness, she surely felt the burden of raising nine kids on her own. Soon after that, we moved to Danville, and I attended George Washington High School. I met a young man and became pregnant. I was only sixteen and had the baby at seventeen. I started to be rebellious, both toward God and toward my mother.

I began hanging out with people who showed me how to steal. I began to shoplift. In my twenties, I was introduced to drugs. Someone approached me and asked me to try cocaine. I knew the person, and I said no. But then, he was someone I knew well and trusted, and since I trusted him, I thought, *Why not?*

That day, I began a destructive path that lasted for many years. I was in and out of jail. My mother, with the help of Benny's mother, raised my daughter.

There will come a time when God is getting ready to set up the process, and it will look like it's not God. An example of this was a time in my life when I ended up with a sentence of six months in jail even though I was innocent of the charge. I was upset, had no hope, and had just given up.

I was lying in bed one weeknight when a lady from Good News Ministry, Mrs. Joanne Nester, came in to do jail ministry. I had seen her during my previous incarcerations but never paid any attention to her. I just focused on doing my time and getting out. I acted differently than I had when I was in jail before.

I wasn't disrespectful to the officers, and I didn't fight them. I just stayed to myself. But on this night around 6:00 p.m., she started to sing. I could hear and feel love. I knew God and loved Him.

But I hadn't experienced God's love and grace like I did on that night. I got up and went up to the table and began to weep. I gave it all to God, my past and future, and God received me. From that day until this day, I have been redeemed. God's love brought me through and still does. That was fifteen years ago.

I can relate to our youth today when they make a mistake. I want to let them know God is love. God is forgiving. God's love reaches high. God's love goes low. He will come to you. God will forgive you no matter what you have done or said. I became a new creature in the Danville City Jail. It wasn't just emotion because I'm still set free and delivered. His love keeps me.

Years later, here I am, set free from all bondage. Though I was raised in church, I have lived a rebellious life. I thought I would always be on drugs and could never change.

But now, I'm here to testify that God is a deliverer.

There is nothing you may be involved in that God can't bring you out of. I'm built for this! I know how to help troubled young people because I know how God rescued me.

God has given me the answers as to how to reach out and how to help the children. Because of my past struggles, I have a way to talk to them. God has brought me out of my past; therefore, they can believe that He can bring them out too. Some of them call me daily. I make school visits. I go to certain areas every day and check on them.

I am built for this. My former disobedience helps me to be obedient. I lived a life of being deceived by the devil, thinking that things of the world were cool and wouldn't hurt me. I was wrong. My testimony is that there is nothing too hard for God. And I tell it with thankfulness and trust in the power of His might.

I love this ministry because I don't want these young people to get caught in the devil's trap. I don't want them to try drugs, to fight, or murder anyone. I tell them that the devil comes to steal, kill, and destroy. But Jesus comes that we may have life abundantly. I tell them not to be tricked by the enemy. Love hides a multitude of sins.

Me and my first born the one I had at 17

CHAPTER 6

SOLIDER IN THE ARMY OF THE LORD

"Man, that lady must be crazy."

"Who does she think she is?"

"Those kids are not going to change," a man with slick tongue laughed.

Voices of defeat echoed in my ear every day. But God, a lot of days people would come to see if what I was doing was real. Is this really happening? When spectators came out, they could see that God's plan was actually happening. *God is using me to change the atmosphere.*

Honestly, at the very beginning, there were things I had to learn. I had to relearn the streets and assist the kids on learning positive alternatives to the streets.

My vision was to show love. I wanted His presence to be felt every step of the way. I also wanted others to be encouraged by faith walk. I knew the vision and path being set for me was a chosen one. I wanted to encourage others to listen to His voice.

Sometimes, I would be alone in my faith walk. I would go to the park and pray all around the park. Then, there were times I would have mighty women of God with me. We commanded that evil be bound in His precious and mighty name. We cried out to God! *We wanted love, love to be felt all over the park.*

One day, I prayed to God and asked Him what I should do with all of the gang members we had.

God said, *They are a group of young men who have lost their way. It takes a group to carry out the devil's plans. But I will use a different group to cancel it. Be not afraid.*

His voice soothed my fears and gave me boldness. I knew the path I needed to take. I was going to do what He instructed me to do. By His power, I would do the ministry. There were days I would get to the park and did not know what to expect. I would step out with a clean heart, open to everyone. I lived in the expectation for God to have prepared my way. I was not afraid of the atmosphere or the youth. I approached them with a smile. I opened my mouth knowing God would speak for me, as He always does on my behalf.

God used the game of basketball as a bait to get their attention. If God tells you to fish with potato salad, then cook it and cast it in the net. God takes the things that are foolish to us to confound the enemy.

Me and a few gang members I was working to help
them leave that behind them. Helped one graduate with
his GED he dropped out of high school at 17.

CHAPTER 7
CASTING HIS NET

"Hey, have you seen Neal?" I would ask.

I would look for some kids, hoping to see them again. If they did not show up again, I would pray for them. I wanted them to feel the love of God wherever they were in the world. There were days that I would get a lot of help, and there were days that I would have no help.

I had no help. Either way, I kept going. During the first four weeks, I was going to the park on Tuesdays and Thursdays.

From day to day, I never knew what to expect. However, I kept going. This is what God wanted.

I remember praying, crying, and fasting for God to keep me in His will. I was new to all of this. I needed Him to carry me every step of the way. Some days, I felt like I was being watched by the kids and people around me. I felt like I was being judged. I knew that they might be wary of my intentions.

I said, *"Lord, let them always see You."*

I absolutely prayed without ceasing. I had to stay in the spirit. In the beginning, transportation was a huge problem. But God always made a way.

"Take me on through, God." I would pray. God answered my prayer when we were invited to an event for Hoop Don't Shoot at New Life Community Church. And praise God. Mr. Kenny Lewis, a retired NFL football player, was the guest speaker.

The pastor's wife, Mrs. Stephanie Reed, was there that night. Afterward, she approached me and said God had laid it on her heart to be a blessing to Hoop Don't Shoot. A date was set for a couple of young men and me to come to the church service and testify about the program. The time came for them to give their testimony. The whole ministry was such a blessing. Their congregation showed us so much love. We were able to obtain transportation through their giving, and enough money to carry us for the entire year.

We were so grateful to them and Pastor Reed for having us and blessing us in such an overflow. They also sponsored a big tournament with Pastor Nathan Williams speaking. Twenty-one youth were saved! God loves unity. He was changing lives, and opportunities made possible through Hoop Don't Shoot.

My heart jumps and leaps for joy on a daily basis when we ride in the Hoop Don't Shoot van. This is our second one. The first one, a donated one, broke down, but it lasted us a full year.

After we left New Life Church me and my daughter went
out to eat with Pastor Jim and Mrs. Stephanie.

CHAPTER 8

THE ROSE THAT GREW FROM CONCRETE

"I am not a punk. You better get off my face," said boy number one.

"Man, keep running your mouth. I will make you eat those words and take them back to your nappy-headed Mama. Wait, don't worry. I will tell her tonight when I see her," he said with a smirk on his face.

The friction between the boys playing mirrored the friction between the hot asphalt and their shoes. Things could get mighty tense between the players.

I never had a class on at-risk youth or gangs before I started Hoop Don't Shoot.

I just had a calling from the Lord that something must be done to stop the evil that was happening with the killings in my area. I have had to learn many things on the "fly."

I thank God that He has protected me in my ignorance and has given me courage to face the challenges head on in His strength. I am always learning something new from these kids, and then, I work to apply it the next situation.

This day was one of those situations where I learned a very important lesson.

"Stop it right now! You know I don't tolerate fighting out here!" My voice was drowned out by the yelling, cussing, and fists that were swinging through the air. Sweat was flying all over, and bodies were wrestling on the ground as two sixteen-year-old young men fought it out.

The day had been so hot. Tempers were flaring all day long. I had already had to get in between the guys several times. I should have probably just shut it down, but I was giving everybody grace because of the weather. The heat definitely has a way of making the guys more agitated. I don't cancel those days though because the goal is to keep them from doing something bad somewhere else, and Hoop Don't Shoot is here as a good activity for that reason. So we push on humidity, heat, and all.

"You grab him, and I'll help grab this one!" I shouted.

"Knock it off right you two, or I'm going to suspend you from Hoop Don't Shoot! Y'all better get a hold of yourselves! Push him that way and get the other guy over there. We got to let them cool off."

Before I knew what was happening, the boy went running to the area where they set all of their backpacks and he started yelling, "I'm going to shoot you!"

He said to the other young man, "Right now, I'm sick of you! I'll kill you now!"

My heart dropped as I realized he was running for his backpack to get his gun out of it. I had no idea before then that he was carrying a gun in there, but it was obvious that's what he meant. Everyone started running and trying to get to him before he got to his backpack.

Everything happened so fast. When I looked up, I saw this young man grabbing different backpacks. He seemed frustrated and started yelling, "No, you didn't! Who stole my backpack? I set it right over here. My phone and gun were in there! Where is it? Somebody better start talking now!"

I couldn't have been more relieved but was still very nervous because what if it was over there still. He looked and looked and never found it. He stormed off, and I was thankful. We shut down for the rest of the day.

God had protected us from a very dangerous, deadly situation once again. The backpack never turned up. I still don't know if one of the kids, who knew he had the gun, took it because of the fight or if someone just stole it to take it for themselves. To me, it was an angel protecting all of us from the temper of a young man with a deadly weapon. The young man didn't realize it then, but God had protected him from doing something that day that he would have regretted the rest of his life.

When I grew up, we carried books, pencils, crayons, and paper in our backpacks. I was ignorant to what was being carried in the backpacks of our Hoop Don't Shoot youth, but I quickly learned backpacks are for tennis shoes and guns. We check backpacks now, and I didn't let my ignorance stop me but instead, learned from the lesson and pushed forward in the name of Jesus. I continue to learn new things everyday as God reveals lessons, learning as I go.

CHAPTER 9
IN THE BEGINNING

We started off with a referee, but after doing Hoop Don't Shoot for two weeks, Minister Price from True Holiness Church came out and refereed for the summer. But he changed jobs and had to leave.

Therefore, I began to referee myself. I didn't know a lot about the game, but being a spiritual lady, I could tell when the guys were getting angry. I would step in and pray or start calling Jesus's name, and everything would chill.

At the beginning, I had around four fights, but after a lot of prayer, consistency, and a lot of love, the atmosphere changed. And the young guys changed. After seeing I wasn't going anywhere, they began to trust me and talk to me more. They even began to confide in me. We have not had another fight in more than a year.

About a year into Hoop Don't Shoot, I began to see an increase in young ladies and girls coming to Hoop Don't Shoot. Mrs. Joyce Mayo, who started with me, helped me in so many ways. She inspired me and helped me all through the first summer. She organized a cheerleader group of girls which was so amazing. But she also had to leave me. Some days, I would be all by myself with fifty youth.

By the grace of God, I stayed focused and continued to have Hoop Don't Shoot Tuesdays and Thursdays. *I would stand out there at park and pray, "God send me some help!* Not just any help but someone with love in their hearts for Your children, God."

Someone who can take this heat. Yes, it was one hundred degrees some days. I need someone who will help me build Your kingdom and not judge them or me.

Some people came only to judge me and the kids, not realizing that if they would help me, God would help them. I was and still am on an assignment from God to show love to His children and to introduce Him to them.

We can't look at the place and say, "This is not of God."

We can't look at the people and say, "They are not God's."

I have learned that God will set a platform anywhere. All he needs is a willing, bold soul to say, "Yes!"

If I looked at my atmosphere and the people, I would sink like Peter walking on the water to get to Jesus. We have to look up to the hills from whence comes our help. We have to trust Him and not faint. I can't say I don't, sometimes, get a little weary. I do.

I cry a lot for the young souls. I pray a lot for their deliverance. I pray that they grab hold to God and to His love for them.

I'll say, "Lord, lead me, guide me, and speak through me. Use me, Lord." I am always available to Christ my Lord.

I use Christian music as one of the means to change the atmosphere. I always plan and only play gospel music on the radio, and some of them have never heard Christian music before. I play the gospel songs and sing sometimes.

As time has passed, the boys have started singing with them and clapping. When I hear the singing along with the music, we sing together in unity, and sometimes, I will pull over and we get out and praise God.

This has inspired them to learn to say, "I'm sorry" to one another.

There are so many ways to introduce Jesus to our youths. I try them all. One song by the *Gospel Legends* is called "Repent of Your Sins and Be Baptized." *It is a song that helps me on my day-to-day journey.*

The Holy Spirit lets me know I had gang members. I publicly addressed the situation. "I know that some of you are in gangs. You are still welcome to come play with us."

From that day to this day, they continue to come. God has changed lives. Some we lost to incarceration. But they are still alive. I continue to tell them that God still loves them. God will not forget them.

As summer passed, I became worried about the program. It was challenging to play basketball on an outdoor court on a dark, cold, winter days. Then, one late summer day, a young lady from the Danville Parks and Recreation came to Hoop Don't Shoot. She invited us to use the Danville City Auditorium when it became too cold to play at the Park. What a relief. God was constantly preparing and making a way for us!

I throw the ball up at least 1000 times in the name of Jesus

CHAPTER 10

A CHANGE IS COMING

The first year of Hoop Don't Shoot, we had visitors from all over Danville, who came out to support the youth. They would join us in prayer and help out. I would tell the young men, "Be good. We have company," as if we were at home.

Some of them behaved and some couldn't. Some had never been shown how to love and how not to say something that would hurt a brother or sister. As I walked and talked and prayed around the park with them, I heard a lot of negative talk about each other's clothes, shoes, and hair.

I began to pray at that moment and called on Jesus to help them change their hearts. The ones talking about the others were often neighbors and were in the same shoes, so to speak. They just talked about each other to make them feel better about themselves. I would hug them so close.

They would have an outburst when they lost a game. You would have thought someone had hit them. But the youth were expressing anger from some other's hurt.

I would say, "Son, God loves you. Son, calm down." I would speak with a calm voice. God had given me His Spirit. The fruit of His Spirit is love, kindness, and patience.

At Hoop Don't Shoot, I can see where the atmosphere has changed. They walk away from confrontations. They don't always respond now. I give God all the glory. Sometimes, it is so special to be at Hoop Don't Shoot and not hear a cross word.

"Peace be still" is what God has granted to us. Peace in the valley. His joy in our storm.

I'll never forget after speaking about Hoop Don't Shoot, one man followed me and asked, "Lady, is you crazy?" I smiled and kept walking. I knew His plan was mightier than any ridicule or criticism I could encounter.

Playing the game

CHAPTER 11
I WILL TRUST IN THE LORD

I have known heartbreak, yes. But I have also known joy.

"Lord, this is Your ministry; Your will be done. These are Your children. We are the sheep of Your pasture. Lord, let Your will be done."

I have this to say, everybody is not going to be for you. And not everyone will encourage you. If it is God's will, I know He will finish what He started. All I have to do is keep trusting, keep pushing, and keep pressing! I need to show up, even when I am by myself. All we have to do is show up. God will do the rest.

I went in full force, not once a week but twice. Let's get to know God. Let's get to know one another. What I couldn't take care of, God did. My whole schedule changed. My whole life changed. I was in it to win souls for God.

I noticed that when I would call for prayer, there were many who wouldn't come to the circle. I didn't force them. They had to understand my intentions. They watched me. They studied me. Some would ask me different questions. As time passed, they joined us, and we all were praying.

How do I handle all of them? The Holy Spirit does. I can tell when they are happy, sad, or mad. The Holy Spirit tells me how to handle them and how to calm them without calling the police. If I called the police, they would come and lock them up. I want to show them how to let go and let God fight their battles; don't fight your brother.

Before anyone judges them, they should take a look at what they were going through. Look at their surroundings. Look at the pressure just to be a youth these days. And I notice a lot of our youth have no hope. They have given up. The devil has taken hope from them. But I came to tell them that God is hope. God is love. You will live and not die. I often speak that to them. You will live and not die. God is with you.

I have stories of success, and I have stories of heartbreak. At the beginning of school, we prayed our students would have a good year. We went to the city auditorium, and we kept our routine. Aglow came with us. Once every month, they brought the kids snacks and drinks. We would play two games and have a speaker.

Hoop Don't Shoot has a tremendous impact on many young people. WSET News and other news outlets interviewed participants.

Students' grades have improved. In addition, students are receiving less disciplinary referrals. Some of the young men have received jobs. Members of the First Pentecostal Church assisted them in writing a resume. Several of them obtained jobs in their local community. As I aforementioned earlier, we have had several of the young men enter military careers also. This makes me happy. I am glad that these young men will get to see the world and learn new skills.

One evening, we were leaving a basketball tournament at the park. A young man confided in me that he wanted to be dropped off last. After dropping off all the other youth, he told me he wanted me to help him get a job. I pulled the car over and began to pray and cry out to God for him. I asked God to help me to help him.

I knew it would be a hard task because I could tell by his tattoos that he had spent time in jail. He had a tattoo on his face also. I became very close to him. I had him with me almost every day. We went to interview after interview. And bless his heart, he wore a necktie and dress clothes. He wanted to obtain employment. He wanted to be productive, to be a man with ambition. I could see the change in his attitude and his faith in God. He would join me in church, clapping his hands.

One Sunday, he joined. The angels rejoiced and so did I! He went back to school and was doing well. Until one day, he couldn't fight his demons, and he didn't call me. He left school early and went back into the gang. He will have to confess to God and ask for forgiveness and ask Him to give him a clean heart. Hopefully, a seed was planted through Hoop Don't Shoot that will bring him back to God.

We have so many praise reports. At the beginning of 2018, two young men began to think about obtaining a GED. One day, I was prompted in my spirit to ask at Hoop Don't Shoot if anyone wanted to go get their GED. To my surprise, four or five hands went up. We had already been invited to attend the school on Jefferson Street by the founder. She had come by with applications earlier that summer. In my heart, I knew it was time to act on her purpose. I took two of my players to the GED school that morning at 10:00 a.m. When we arrived, they asked me to go with them. I laughed. Oh, no! I had no interest in going back to school. But I had testified earlier that I had also dropped out of school at the age of sixteen.

I knew if my dad were still alive, I would have never dropped out. I sat in the car for a minute and so did they. And then, out of my love for them, I said, "Let's go." We went to school together. I'm so proud of one of my particular players. He went on to graduate.

He got his GED diploma at Langston High School. He went across the stage with a big smile and a dance of achievement. Again, I cried. His close friend was there; The students and his parents and even the mayor attended. We shared a dinner at the Jefferson Street school.

To this day, his picture wearing his cap and gown is up in the schoolhouse. I am still in the GED class, learning basics. I will graduate, and I have two youth attending with me.

When I began Hoop Don't Shoot, I never ever thought I would be mother, father, mentor, and confidant to these young men. I didn't know when I stepped out into the deep end that God would give me a net full. On any particular day, I would go from school to job interviews, to pray, to eat, and to a school visit.

I would get up to ten calls a day. "Ms. Angie, where you at?"

"Ms. Angie, what are you doing?"

"Ms. Angie, can you bring me something to eat?"

"Ms. Angie, can you pray for me over the phone? I'm having a bad day." I stand in the gap for them.

I'm a firm believer that if you believe in the vision, you believe in the process, and you believe in God more than yourself, anything is possible. Many of the former participants have gone to service and or are employed. All of this is a testament to God's grace and mercy.

Many parents worry about their kids and social media. Many parents don't check their sites. Some problems start on social media. It is important that you monitor their sites and actions. It is not a bad idea to limit their participation on social media. I have had parents tell me how they feel lost. They don't know what to do or expect from their children. They have given them guidance, resources, and love. Yet they still want to get involved in negative activities. Social media can be used for good and bad purposes. That is why it is wise to monitor their usage. Talk to them about bullying and other negative behaviors. Ask them questions.

You might feel that you are nagging them. However, you are actually helping them. They might be mad at you, but you both will be glad in the long run.

Playing the game

CHAPTER 12

CLOSE CALLS

"Hey, I'm going to roll through Green Street and see if I can find some kids wanting to come to Hoop Don't Shoot. I'll be back later," I said as I backed the van out of my driveway.

The sun was shining bright, and I had my gospel music bumpin'. It was a good day.

"Lord, I'm praying you would show me who to minister to today. I'm going drive around my usual spots, but you bring who you want. You draw them. You have been so good. You make a way out of no way. I'm counting on you to help me reach these kids today. Save them, Lord Jesus!"

As I drew closer to the park, I saw the police and a bunch of my kids standing around. My heart started beating faster. *Oh no, Lord, please don't let anyone be shot! Please don't let one of our kids be the one who did it! No, Lord!*

As I took in the scene, that's exactly what my first thoughts were. I can't help it. That's just where they go because of the many experiences I've already witnessed with kids killing kids. Sure enough, I get out of my car and start walking over. I see the police with one of our Hoop Don't Shoot kids, and my heart just sunk. "What's going on? What happened?" I asked the eight-year-old boy standing in front of the cops.

This kid's tears began to flow as soon as I called his name, and our eyes met. He knew I cared about him and would do whatever I could to help him, and he was in some serious trouble.

"Ma'am, do you know this young man?" the cops asked me.

"Yes, I know him. He's one of my Hoop Don't Shoot kids. Officer, can you tell me what in the world he did? He's only eight."

"Well, today, he was with another eight-year-old boy, and they pulled out a homemade gun on the people at the house they were at. And it looked so real, the owner went to get his gun. We were called because everyone thought the gun was real. They could have both been killed! This is very serious, Ma'am. We're trying to figure out what exactly we are going to do seeing as he is only eight."

"Sir, I will call his mom right now. I know her."

I called her up, told her son had made a fake gun and pulled it on people, and then I asked her if I could take him home.

"Please, Miss Angie, bring him home. I don't know what I'm going do with that boy!"

"His mama said I could take him home," I told the officer.

"No, ma'am, we will be escorting him home in the police car. He needs to learn a lesson, and we are hoping this will scare him enough. We have to let him know this was very serious. We can't have him doing this again. The next time he might not be so lucky."

As the cop car pulled away from the curb, tears filled my eyes as I looked at child, just a young boy, sitting in the back of the police car. He should be having a ride for fun, not for having done something so bad. This isn't how it should be, Lord! In that moment though, I thank God right there that both of their lives had been spared. It was only the grace of God that had protected him.

The situation could have been much worse. Once again, I was thankful I was there for the kids, and I hoped that a life lesson had been learned and that wouldn't repeat itself. I'm happy to say that the young man is still at Hoop Don't Shoot, and he hasn't had another ride in a cop car since.

I also receive calls from kids who are contemplating suicide. I am working with churches to bring in counselors for these kids. There are so many issues that these kids go through. Instead of judging them, it is my duty to help them.

CHAPTER 13
BUILDING BRIDGES

When we left the city auditorium during the spring of 2018, we began the second summer of Hoop Don't Shoot. We had some youth who had been with us for a while and new ones joined.

We enjoyed games and speakers. Aglow held a wonderful anniversary banquet at the River Church of God for us.

Sergeant Neal brought new trainees for the police department, and they played basketball with us the whole summer. We helped these police officers to be accepted. They brought water, T-shirts, and jerseys for us.

We enjoyed that so much. I saw them interact with the youth and build relationships, and it was real. They are genuine people with big hearts. They prayed with us and for us. All I can say is, they serve God.

One day, we had a fire here in Danville. A family lost everything they had. We had two young ladies from the neighborhood, who did not have a lot themselves, bring some of their own belongings to me to give to the family. God's love was helping us change. I saw a lot more compassion being shown.

God sent a businessman, Mr. Stuart Smith, to assist us. He organized a crowdfunding on social media. He was able to raise three thousand dollars. He used it to supply us with water, T-shirts, and pizza every Thursday. At the end of the summer, he gave us a banquet at SkateTown.

He gave a trophy to all attendees. What a heart!

Five weeks later, Compassion Church joined us. We prayed together. They also taught younger kids on Thursdays.

We also had several volunteers. Shakeva Fraizer is one of those volunteers. She has had a huge impact on our ministry. We had a lot of churches join us in prayer. The community was truly helping us build bridges.

Mr. Steven Darr, from Charlottesville, was also a blessing to us. He treated the Hoop Don't Shoot Program to a Duke Game. We were also treated to dinner. It was an awesome experience for the kids.

We were honored by Aglow Lighthouse with a Valentine's Day party for our girls that participated in the program. It was held a Lively Stones Baptist Church, located in Pelham, North Carolina. Aglow also held a wonderful anniversary banquet at the River Church of God for us.

Barry Inge has been a very big assistance to me. He helps the kids with their homework.

He also referees games. He helps wherever he is needed. Pastor and Mrs. Shawn Giese are also faithful. He does discipleship classes with the kids.

Ms. Deborah Giese, Stevette Anderson, Starlette Hardy, and Rhynecor Inge have been instrumental in the program. I value and appreciate all that they have done to assist me and the kids. Ms. Hardy brings kids to her home. She cooks the most tasty meals. She taught them how to sew and make Bible covers.

Police officer playing with the boys and Glo giving
away Christmas gifts at the city auditorium.

CHAPTER 14
MURDERS IN DANVILLE

On days of a murder, here in Danville would be a tense day at Hoop Don't Shoot. I would have to pray with my ma or friends in Christ before I would go. If the murder occurred on the Northside of town, I'd have to watch them, or if the Southside, I'll have to watch them.

They'll come gather in gangs and talk. I'll go over in the middle of then and ask is everything alright. And I can tell the aggressor of the group. I'll talk and pray with them. When we gather in the circle to pray as a group, I'll bring it up in front of everyone. Put the devil out. And let them know, please don't retaliate. I'll bring up prison, and their parents will be hurt.

Those days, I'll speak longer to them and at the same time, be in tears. A lot of times you can tell their feeling some kind of bad way. The whole gang, ten young men, will wear the dead individual on their shirt and looking mean. I'll say, *Okay, Jesus. We have one of these days.*

On some days, they'll bring the beef from school to Hoop Don't Shoot. I listen to them talk in the car sometimes, and sometimes, I'll get the info from school. And I'll bring it up and pray, and they'll have it in their mind to finish the fight regardless. So here I go.

I often get between them, and I thank God for the anointing. I can talk and pray them out of fighting, to let go of hate. I'll say the consequences are really high. By the grace of God, no one has gotten hurt or killed.

One night while resting in bed, listening to the sleet pop across the window, I received a call from a young man. He had been a part of the Hoop Don't Shoot for two years. We became really close. He confided a lot to me. At that time, I did a lot of one-on-one talks with him. I knew that he wanted out of the gang lifestyle.

At that time, I had lost two participants to incarceration. I constantly reminded him how God was sparing his life to live and be free. So I kept going the extra mile to keep him safe.

"Ms. Angie, come get me before I kill my friend."

I said, "What?"

He explained his situation to me. I knew he had an anger issue.

I said, "Let me get up. Lord, take the wheel."

I did not want another murder in Danville.

I went to pick him up. I talked to him all the way home. He went with me to church the following Sunday. We talked about forgiveness. A couple of weeks later, he and the other young man became friends again.

Praying

CHAPTER 15

SOMETHING MIRACULOUS HAPPENED

The work of the Holy Spirit is amazing. After fellowshipping with First Pentecostal Church, I went home one Saturday morning. I was mowing my grass. The Holy Spirit spoke to me.

"I am ready to do something marvelous in your life."

And behold, I walked into the kitchen. My phone was ringing. It was my sister and friend in Christ, Mary, from Aglow International, here in Danville, Virginia.

"Angie, how would you like to go to Spokane, Washington?"

I replied, "How would we get there?"

She said, "Fly."

I responded, "No."

The International Leadership for Aglow was asking us to go to the West Coast to do an interview about Hoop Don't Shoot. Initially, I thought I would send a video. My mother was sitting at the table, listening to the conversation. She was adamant that I go on the trip. It is always my goal to honor my mother wishes. Therefore, I made the decision to go on the trip. The Aglow team paid for all of my traveling expenses. I had delicious meal. My entire experience was first class.

I had an experience with God in worship that I had never experienced before in my life. My heart leaps when I reminisce about my first trip. Thank you, Aglow Light House, for having me to go to

Spokane to discuss Hoop Don't Shoot. There is a video on YouTube in reference to the interview.

Hoop Don't Shoot ministry gets hard at times. I pray a lot, and I also cry a lot. God has made a way for me, every step of the way. I've seen God send people, resources, and supplies to assist me. I have also seen God remove people that did not have good intentions for the program. God has sent churches, community leaders, and citizens of Danville to often lend me a hand.

My mother, Leola Johnson, has been my supporter. She is always by my side: We are always together. She encourages me to be my best. She loves the Hoop Don't Shoot Ministry. She is my praying partner and confidant. Often, the youth will come by and chat with her. My daughter, Zion, is also one of my biggest supporters. She is actually the person that named the ministry Hoop Don't Shoot. Zion has been a constant source of encouragement to me. She does not get jealous of the time I spend with other kids. She understands my calling. She also prays with me. All of my daughters have supported my efforts. They have assisted me in projects. I love them for just being them.

CHAPTER 16
THE BEST IS YET TO COME

I can truly say that God is in this ministry. I often get text messages from the kids. They might state that they are going to church. I go around Sunday mornings, picking up the kids.

My heart is overjoyed!

I pray every day that the strongholds in their lives be released. I want them to walk freely and boldly in their freedom.

Other times, someone might call me, requesting prayer. They know that there is power in the name of Jesus. Before every game, with prayer, I pray for them when they are in pain, depressed, or hurting. We have become a family.

I see that God is using Hoop Don't Shot as a way of showing the kids how to escape situations that they don't know how to get out of.

I want them to know that God loves them. They need to know that they matter in this world. I want them to feel love.

I don't compromise with the devil. I play gospel music. I am also constantly saying His praises. They need to know my relationship with God is real. I have to be firm and consistent.

They can change if I don't change.

I have purchased school clothes, food, and haircuts. Anything I can do; I will do it to help them. Some of them have confided in me. They have stopped stealing or smoking drugs. God is getting the victory. *This is His ministry.* I will continue to do His Will. I appreciate everyone who continues or has taken this walk of faith with me. My God bless you!

I thank God for all of my daughters. I am especially grateful for my daughter, Zion. As I stated, she is the person that named Hoop Don't Shoot. She is being a great source of love and support. She helps me organize and get items. She roots me on. When I grow weary, she uplifts me. It is great to have someone in your corner.

CHAPTER 17
GOD IS STILL ABLE

I know God is a deliverer. I know God is the way out. I know God can change anyone. I know this because I have read His word. I know God is love. I know God daily forgives us for our transgressions. The same way he brought me out, and I know He is able to do it for them.

One day, I was at the kitchen table, and I had just finished eating. My phone rang from the messenger app, and I knew it as probably one of the kids in the program.

The voice on the other end roared, "Ms. Angie!" I was familiar with the voice on the other end. I had previously told him that if he needed me to call me. He was generally a calm kid with a good disposition. He was always respectful. However, the voice on the phone was not calm.

The young man said, "My life is in danger!"

I was completely shocked. This young man was never in trouble. He stated that he helped someone in a fight. Now, someone was after him. I advised him to call the police. He refused to call them. He did not want to snitch. He thought it would cause more trouble. He needed to get out of town, fast!

I drove the young man to a location. A family member picked him up. I have never heard from him again.

In the past, I have stolen items. I stole when I was hungry and barely had anything to my name. I never thought I would have someone steal from me who I had helped. There was a family I had helped a lot. I made sure the kids in the family received haircuts, clothes, and hairstyles. My oldest daughter, who loves to help others, assist me with providing some essentials for the kids. I was worried that they would be bullied in school if they did not have haircuts, clothes, and etc. Therefore, I had to quickly put my plan into action. In a week's time, I had all three of them prepared for school. Often, I make sure that the kids in the program have what they need.

The consult with the board in reference to these matters. We feel that it is important that the kids have what they need to severe incidents as bullying and suicide. We had done our best to make sure that the kids had what they needed. That is why I was so shocked that one of them had stolen from me.

I had fed him, gotten him a haircut, and given him clothes. Honestly, I was hurt. I had spoken to someone who stated the young man was heavily smoking weed. I immediately forgave him. I recalled all the Jesus had done for me. I remembered all the time that he had forgiven me.

I did not put him out of the program. I kept him in prayer and showed him love. There was another time he stole from me. This time, I had to give him a consequence. It hurts me to do so. I was scared I would lose him to the streets.

Sometime later, I was driving in my car. I saw him, his brother, and another young man walking down the street. They had items in hand that I thought did not belong to them. I blew the horn to alert them to the fact that I had noticed them. Later, they were caught and placed in the detention center. I recall crying over them. I was already dealing with another situation with a member. I was comforted by a player.

The young man said, "Ms. Angie, you can't save them all."

One of the participants in the group was a charismatic young man. I will call Paul. I had to suspend him, one time, due to an altercation. He had taken an item from another player. I do not tolerate that kind of behavior.

Eventually, I allowed him back into the program. I always give kids another opportunity to come back to the program. I don't give up on them. I love them like Jesus loves me. He kept giving me chances.

This young man became an active member in Hoops Don't Shoot. I took up for him. We began to talk a lot. He shared his past with me. I did not judge him.

I recall one night he startled me with some news.

"Ms. Angie, I don't want to rob no one else."

I cried, "Son, you don't have to do it no more. I will help you."

I helped him and several other of the boys find jobs pulling tobacco for two months. I also took him to a job interview at a fast-food restaurant. He wanted out of his old lifestyle. He wanted change.

I knew when he told me that he did not want to rob anymore. I knew then that he was not a robber. He robbed to hurt. I could feel the darkness coming from him. I knew the dark side was making him do things. He was tired.

During the summer, we kept playing basketball. We also had a lot of speakers. He listened and even started going to church. We kept in contact. I kept up with him. Anytime I called him, he would answer. When school started, I took him to get registered for school. He was sent to an alternative program. I met his mother. It was clear to see that she loves him. However, he never mentioned his dad. That is the case of many of the kids in Hoops Don't Shoot. I meet their mothers but never see their dads.

A month into the school year of 2018, everything appeared to be going well with him. I received a call from Paul. He wanted me to pick him up. It was not a street that I would normally pick up him from. I was a little puzzled.

I asked, "Why are you not at school?"

He did not respond. He looked very bleak. In my spirit, I knew something was wrong. I kept talking, but he was quiet.

I told him, "I love you, son. Be good, son." He did not respond.

I went to the park the next day to check on the kids. If they are not at the park, I will go to their homes. As I was pulling off, another Hoop Don's Shoot member came to my car.

"Ms. Angie, someone just got shot in front of my house."

I got as close to the murder scene as I could. I prayed that none of my players were shot. I began to pray. Next, I called as many players as I could. I called Paul; he did not immediately answer. However, he later answered. All of my boys were accounted for. I felt a sense of relief. Little did I know, it was short-lived.

However, I was hurt for the young man who was killed. I didn't know him. I was still upset that his life had been taken.

Then next, people were calling me, telling me that Paul had been picked up for murder. I was in total disbelief. I broke down, crying.

My mother asked "What was wrong?"

She tried to console me. I could not believe it. I went to the park. All of the kids were talking about it. I was in denial.

"He did not do it!" I said. We went to the River Church for prayer. Pastor Poe prayed for us. Not only was I heartbroken, a lot of the youth were also sad. The next Sunday, Pastor Poe and Pastor Murray prayed with us. A week later, the kids and I still needed to be console. Mrs. Mary Barnes and I tried to console them.

The incident made me work harder to save the youth. I was more dedicated than ever to make sure that these kids knew that I believed in them. I wanted them to know that God loved them and could change them. I wanted them to know that life can get better. They just needed to hold on to God and believe.

I wanted them to know that I would be there for them.

I started to make sure that more of the kids had jobs. I saw an advertisement in a local newspaper. I saw that a farmer was paying $10/hour to chop weeds from around the tobacco stalks. I mentioned it to the kids one day. Several showed interest. The next morning, I got up at 5:00 a.m. to pick up several of them.

They were not familiar with the process of working in a tobacco farm. They had on tank tops, slides, and etc. I knew that they needed to wear different clothing and shoes. Our day was long. Many of them complained. Some quit and got in the van. We worked until 12:00 p.m.

Several of them were still willing to work. Therefore, I got up early in the morning to make sure that they had money to purchase school supplies, clothes, and etc. It was a learning experience for all of us. Different tempers, mixed with heat, caused a few arguments with the supervisor. I had to calm down both parties. We worked about a month. The smile they had on their faces when they received their checks were worth it. They were proud that they were able to purchase items. They were proud of their own efforts.

Hoop Don't Shoot is the sound of basketballs bouncing. It is the sound of kids cheering each other on to victory. Hoops Don't Shoot is the smiles, love, and laughs we share. I cherish the times I hear "I love you" from the players. My heart rejoices with more love.

The love we share is the breeze on a one hundred degrees day. Hoops Don't Shoot is a happy place and safe place. It is a place to make friends and unwind from a stressful day. We don't discriminate against anyone. It is a place where you can find drinks, snacks, and a loving, caring arm. We are family.

We also provide tutoring and homework services for our youth. We have many kids in the program that are very smart. They just need guidance and some help to get to the next level in life.

CHAPTER 18
MY REASON

Kenndy Hamlett started off with me in 2017. He's been a helper to me all the way until the day he was shot. He always cleaned up before and after we had a basketball tournament. I sent pictures of. In 2018, he received his GED through Hoop Don't Shoot and received a job through Hoop Don't Shoot. In 2021, he was walking from getting some food on Piney Forest Rd., and a car drove past him and turned in the road and shot him two times. On that night, we were going a trip to Bush Gardens the next day, and he was going. So we waited for a few minutes for him, but the bus driver was on a schedule so we had to go. On the way back, I was told by another young man he had been shot. I said, "No, not Kenndy," because he was a humble good kid just trying to start his future. So I brushed it off, and two days later, I received a call from him from the hospital saying he had been shot. I began crying and praying and thanking God he's still alive. As of today, he's not walking, but he's still alive. We meet together sometimes. We've bonded in love that's why I do Hoop Don't Shoot.

Kenndy is getting his GED

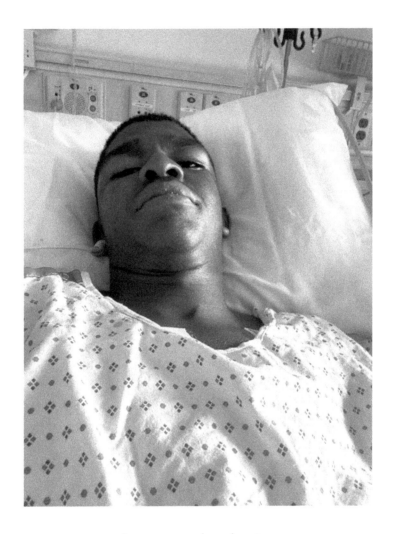

Just was a random shooting

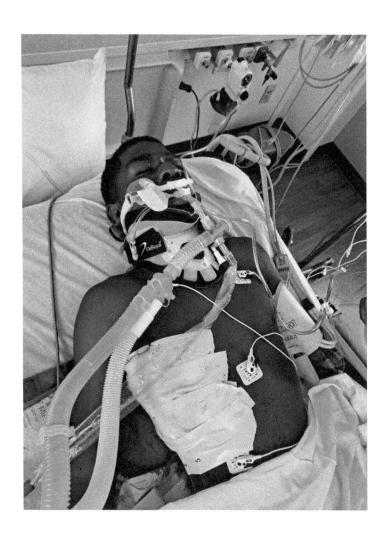

CHAPTER 19
TESTIMONIES

For I know the thoughts that I think toward you, saith the LORD, thoughts of peace, and not of evil, to give you an expected end. Then shall ye call upon me, and ye shall go and pray unto me, and I will hearken unto you. And ye shall seek me, and find me, when ye shall search for me with all your heart. (Jeremiah 29:11–13)

All right, let me be real with you. My name is AKA Smokey. They named me that because I love to smoke weed. I grew up in the hood where you have to learn to live or die. My ma raised me and my four brothers because our father wasn't around. Men came in and out of our lives growing up. I didn't spend much time in the house. I was driven to the block at a young age. Life was a struggle. I started fighting off bullies at the age of twelve. Then, I began disconnecting from my family and joined a gang on my block. We vowed to be there forever, lifetime friends. That decision, I shouldn't have made at such a young age, and now, I am grown and still active.

I dropped out of high school in the tenth grade. It just wasn't for me. To start off, I started smoking weed when I was ten years old. Smoking became a way of living in my household and on the block. As I got older, I began to feel uneasy, seeing guys I went to school with doing good. Seeing them drive nice cars and nice girl. I feel like that's not for me, but I want it. I fell into this, born into this life. I was locked up in them slammers when I turned eighteen for assault and possession of weed. I haven't been back in the last three years since Mrs. Angie came in my life. My tattoos show my pain, people I've lost in the streets. My demons still haunt me. I still do the same things I'm used to doing—stealing from stores, robbing places. I have to let some tides past me by. I'll say no this time.

I feel uncomfortable when Mrs. Angie takes me to church and nice places. I feel judged by the people, but when we get there and the people are nice, I feel better. I'll be standing there saying, *Were do these people come from? Why they care about me?*

I'm not used to it. I've been judged on my appearance, and I'm labeled by where I live in Danville. They don't know how I became to be who I am. When you become used to cursing or being cursed at, fighting and shooting, you see that as a part of life. Then, here comes Mrs. Angie saying, no cursing, no fighting, don't hurt each other than you like. What?

But since the past year, I've become a better young man. I can feel more than hate. I cannot curse around Mrs. Angie. I may fight every now and then. I still try not to. I still yet have to understand this Jesus she talks about. It's hard to believe Mrs. Angie was once me in some ways. She says, sometimes, "I used to fight and shoplift to have clothes."

I couldn't see her like that. She tells us Jesus changed her. Can He change me? Can He save me? I'm a dead man walking, will he stop the bullet from hitting me? It could be the weed. I could be hallucinating. I see myself in the streets, shoot down and going to prison. So many have already gone in front of me. I'll take their charges, and they take mine. We don't break the "bro code," we ride for each other. Not all stand, some fold. The one that is trigger happy, be the one to snitch. No one has folded on me yet. I'm at an age now. I have to stop trying to keep up with the twelves/the police before I leave home. And I'm ready to get a job. I didn't pay a lot of attention in school. This speaker came to HDS from the same block as me, lived the same life I live. We were neighbors when he left and went to the army. When he came back home, he told me that he had stopped making excuses for himself. That stuck with me because I'll always say this, "All I know is why learn now? Why change now?"

But Mrs. Angie wouldn't stop saying we are going back to school together and we did. And it all became easy. I passed test after test. Got my GED in two months. I went and signed up for the Army but could not get into the Army because charges held me back. I still have big dreams; I'll go forward and fall back. On days that I have a feeling that things could go wrong, I'll call Mrs. Angie to pick me up. I'll be already high; she can smell it on me. And she'll say, "You smoking that wacky weed."

I would laugh and say, "Mrs. Angie, you crazy." We have moments off the court. After I hang out with her, I would feel pulled back to the trap house. I call it trap because it's usually one way out. A shooting could pop off or a raid that will send everybody off to jail. A small argument could cause a death in a second. I've seen it and went home. Again, you show no fear and have a drink for your bro. Bury me in blue with a blunt. I have no fear. It could go either way. I have a lot of enemies. I'm from the chop aside. But my goons are on the upside.

We grieve differently. We get high with our bro or sis on the shirt. And we wear them almost daily. So our rivals know who we ride with. I hear the prayer Mrs. Angie does before we play basketball. For God to help us, for us to love one another from both sides. I'm trying to get to know Him on my own. I pray just don't know how to pray. There is something about Mr. Angie. She can change my mood. I be so mad when I get to HDS. Sometimes, I haven't eaten. I can't go in the kitchen, or my ma starts fussing and cursing. Nobody knows the life of me. I failed for a lot of reasons. Then, I get my hopes up to get a job, but I do not get the position. Give it up, I say. Then, go in front of the judge who does not care that I'm hungry.

She has a thug like me applying to get a job. Where's my break? Then, we are posting free my bro because he caught a charge because no one believes or trusts us. We will be the ones to work. Mrs. Angie believes in us. I will get out this hood. I will be a man one day, not a thug. Hoop Don't Shoot really helped me to be a better person. It also helped me to get jobs. Talking with Ms. Angie also helped me with my suicidal thoughts and depression. God bless Ms. Angie and her wonderful organization.

From the start, Hoop Don't Shoot was very influential to me and others. Ms. Angie decided to change the narrative of Danville. I used to fight and want to cuss out people. I learned, in time, to control my anger.

Ms. Angie has a big heart. She will do anything to help anyone. I would recommend you to bring your kids to this program.

Hoop Don't Shoot, if only you can understand what you've done for me for these two years. You made me love basketball. You helped me love the people around me. You made me forget about the struggles around me. You gave me a family. I'll never forget that. I will love you forever.

Ms. Angie, thank you for helping me through my dark times. You showed me that life was worth living. You helped me when I was suicidal and did not want to live anymore. You showed me that I did not need to fight to prove my point. At Hoop Don't Shoot, you teach us that violence is not the answer to our problems. Your program played a huge part of my life. I will always remember you and the program. I love you so much.

From daughter, Zion

Dear Mommy,

I never expected you to be doing the great work you're doing now. I see how focused you are with everything. Hoop Don't Shoot has changed you for the better, and I love it. You're busy every day but somehow, you never make me feel least or forgotten. The sacrifice you make for me and family and still somehow keep a smile on your face is amazing. I cherish very precious time we get, even if you're picking me up. The laughter we share makes me happy. Every day you go out to make the city a better place and am so proud of you for that. You're truly my superwoman. I don't see how you do it all. I know you always get the job done no matter what. Thank you for setting the standards high for me to achieve after you're going. Also, thanks for every time you bucking me in made me dinner. Even when I would wake you up to say, "Bye, Mommy, love you," you still turned over and said, "Bye, bookie. I love you too." Those words took me through the day because I couldn't wait to tell you all about my day. Even though you have meetings, you still listened.

Thank you, bookie.
—Zion Johns

Hoop Don't Shoot Letter
Alex "AJ" Barnette

At first, I was just trying to find a place to play basketball. I didn't know what I was gonna do with my life after high school. When I first came to Hoop Don't Shoot, I had the greatest time of my life, and I met a wonderful Christian woman named Angienette Dixon. And she offered me to play on her team, I accepted. I have been through so much in my life to the point where I was gonna give up on everything, including my own life. The devil was crawling his way through my mind, telling me there's nothing left in my life and that the only thing that I was going to be able to do is lay on my back and die. And the country people, like me, don't make it out of the farms and fields.

I've had thoughts of taking my own life. I needed help badly. I was planning on cutting myself, but the Lord was telling me to call Mrs. Angie and put down the blade and pick up a basketball. Mrs. Angie took time out of her day to come by my house and pray with me, and I felt the Holy Spirit rushing through my veins. I cried and held on to my life. Thanks to Mrs. Angie and Hoop Don't Shoot, my life has completely changed. I am now an army soldier. I'm healthy, I smile a lot more, I play more basketball, and finally, I have the good Lord by my side forever. Thank you, Mrs. Angie and Hoop Don't Shoot for everything.

> God grant me the
> Serenity
> To accept the things I can't change:
> Courage
> To change the things I can:
> and wisdom
> To know the difference

AJ
Barnette

Dear Hoop Don't Shoot,

    If only you can understand what you've done for me for these last two years. You made me love basketball, love the people around me, and made me forget about the struggles around me, and for that, I'm thankful. You made people notice who I was and gave the troubled kids around me dreams that won't ever leave, and again, I'm thankful. Ms. Angie, thank you for giving all of us the opportunity to show out on the court, you gave me a family I'll never forget, and started a legacy that will help kids forever. I love you.

Bryson Jones
AKA
The Truth

Hey, my name is Xavier Smith, and Hoop Don't Shoot has helped me a lot. My grades went up. My connection with God got stronger and better. That's because of this lady named Angienette Dixon. She's a wonderful, intelligent woman. She is the best youth person ever. She helps the youth in a way nobody can. She teaches them a walk with God. River Church is the best church in the world. International glow help her with snacks. They're all great people but most of all, Angie Dixon. She loves me, and you love her back. Support Hoop Don't Shoot.

Love,
Xavier

Dear Ms. Angie,

Thank you for helping me through dark times and showing me that life is worth living. When I first met you, my mind and heart was not in the right place. You helped me find light, where there was darkness, and a way where I thought there was no way. You taught me many things, and for that, I am grateful. You have played a big part in my life, and you are a huge role model for me. Without you, I don't know where I would be right now. You helped me when I was suicidal and didn't want to be here, no fight to prove my point.

I'm glad I found you when I did. You showed me love when I thought there was no love, and you invited me to Hoop Don't Shoot where I got several of support systems, friends, and love. At Hoop Don't Shoot, you teach us that violence is not the answer to our problems, but prayer and God is. Your program had played a big part in my life, and I will always remember you and your program. Thank you so much for everything you taught and showed me. I love you so much.

—Mary

Kaheem Johnson

Hello, my name is Kaheem. Hoop Don't Shoot really help me a lot to better myself as a person and help me get jobs in such time when I was going through depression. And when I had suicidal thoughts, thoughts of taking myself out of hang, but Mrs. Angie came through with the help of God.

It has help me take focuses away from it. I started, with their help, in going back to get my GED, which I am currently working now to accomplished. Also, my plans is to go in the military after get my GED.

God bless Mrs. Angie and this wonderful organization, Hoop Don't Shoot. This means a lot to me and have had a major impact on my life.

From mother

I, Leola Johnson, would like to say how proud I am of my daughter. I stand by her. I always knew from the time she was born, how special she was and only to weigh three pounds. Her struggle came from her childhood, not knowing her biological dad, but was raised by her stepdad. She learned of her dad at the age of fourteen. Through it all, she always called on Jesus, and I and her attended church all her life. After moving to Danville, her stepdad died in a car accident. She started to follow the wrong crowd and was introduced to drugs. But I can say she's a testimony of who and the love of God. And how He can turn people's life around. I'm so thankful for how He delivered my ladybug. I'm so proud of her.

Leola Covington

I hear a lot of excuses why I haven't received help. A lot of people tell me they are afraid of the youth. They're crazy. I see myself, and they need love and guidance to get on track. They need another chance. If you happen to show up to signify, you want her cussing. If they do, they apologize and they pick up on it. It's amazing what love can and will do.

After, we pray the chosen teams after each game. At the beginning, it was hard to get the losers to go up. They get mad if they lose. They're very competitive. But after they pray, I can see the tension leave them. It's a way of showing forgiveness, helping them to grow. Build character. We promote hope. Put fellows back into society. A better youth. A better society.

Each Hoop Don't Shoot is the sound of basketball bouncing. Cheering one another on and smiles shared. Oh, those days when they arrived and come to hug me, and I hear, "I love you, Ms. Angie." Oh, how my heart rejoices. They feel comfortable sharing "I love you" with me and some out loud around the boys. When God do it, it change our hearts.

The love we share is our breeze on a one hundred-degree temperature on a hot day.

Come out and see and feel the transformation. It's a happy place, safe place, and a place to unwind.

To meet up with friends, make new friends, a place to belong to something positive, enjoy snacks, cold drinks, and sometimes, pizza.

Everything free. No fee, just a sign in sheet.

With prayer, then, they play. Then, you hold the games and speak about me. Bring positive and bring life into a dead place.

I went in undercover and dressed in regular clothes, no collar.

My concealed weapon was love.

Just show my love, Angie, God's angel revealed to me.

Love kills a multitude of sin.

Love is who I am.

Through love giving hope!

1. They begin to get their GED.
2. They begin to join the army.
3. Nineteen got baptized at one time
4. Gangs begin to reconciled.
5. They learned to apologize.
6. Their grades and disciplinary change for better.
7. There have been fewer murders.
8. They call me before they fight and shoot.
9. They call me before they commit suicide.
10. Hoop Don't Shoot is love and hope of today.

He took my pain and created who I am, so I can reach the lost, the less fortunate, the ones who has given up hope with felonies, and to help turn the lives around.

God never waste a hurt.

I'm sometimes outnumbered, but on those days, God shows up in a mighty way. His angels take charge. I want to say, I don't get over-whelmed and butterflies with the different unfamiliar spirits, but I've learned to trust God more because He had showed Himself faithful.

You may find yourself in uncomfortable places but being in God's will brings you to submission.

I cannot add up how many times I've threw up the ball in the name of Jesus. It brings so much love and peace because His name is power, no matter where you're at.

In the year 2019 we started a straight program here in Danville, Virginia. At the Danville City Jail, Mr. Mike Mondal help me organized it. Each week, we would bring ten to twenty youth, all ages, on a tour of the jail to help them not to get into trouble. To let them know there's consequences behind their choice. It helps them make the right decision. I know the impact was great. Their response was, "I don't want to come here."

June eleventh

Write about yesterday.

I had a count of 150 youth.

Southside. Hoop Don't Shoot wanted to shout a young man on his way to college in two months. He dropped out in the eighth grade, returned back to school, and graduated. But at the same time, he's caught up in a gang situation. But I see a sweet young man always respectful to all adults. God protected him on. Yesterday, there were multiple guys that wanted to school him. I could feel it in my spirit that the devil was going to show up. And he did. First, it was two gang boys from the Southside. Then, they started calling the rest. About fifteen showed up.

Me and Pastor Shawn started praying over there, and it helped a lot. Because the way they were talking, they wanted to start shouting. I had at least fifty kids there. They got up and walked down the street, still in the park, and as the other guy was leaving, they exposed a gun. Oh my God! I was hollering. I have kids out here. Paster Shawn was behind them. Because he was White, they must have thought he was a undercover police. They got into like four cars and left. They two young men in Hoop Don't Shoot are suspended and can't come back.

When I first heard about the coronavirus and that we will be going on lockdown, no more Hoop Don't Shoot meetings and no more church that they had come to.

I immediately went into prayer. Lord, don't let them get so bored, that their mind wonders to where they think too much. And Lord, don't let no one get hurt.

The next day, I scroll down Facebook. There, I see a sixteen-year-old fighting an eighteen-year-old recording. Lord, please don't let the one that lost go and __ the other. That happens a lot of times. From two weeks not being able to meet to three months. The whole time, I keep in touch with them, all the ladies and gentlemen. We would text or call, or I'll go by and see them to take food.

A lot of them would come over to see me. Some live on my street. During my time, I prayed and read my Bible more and spent a lot of time with family also.

Well, here we are. We got to open on the eleventh of June. Our first day back at Green Street. I and Ms. Kitty went the day before to pray, which I often do, pray before a tournament. I notice during this whole quarantine time, they have been pretty quiet. But by my surprise, they have been beefing through social media. Throwing shoots, not a shot that you're ugly or stink, not a bully shot, and not a shot that I want to fight you, but I'm going to shoot you on sight.

The day of June the eleventh, I began my day. I woke up, talking to Jesus. My spirit revealed to me trouble. I called some prayer warriors to pray. I went around getting snacks, ice, and etc. Then, I started picking up youth. I picked up two loads. When I pulled up, I noticed a crowd already at the court. The reason for the crowd was that we hadn't met in three months. They move to play basketball, so they showed up in five and six and all ages. We begin in prayer, and we always do. I began to speak on, that I pray they all are well and are there to enjoy the day with basketball and love and fun.

I had invited some of the Northside to come. I always invite anyone who want to come to play basketball and hear the speaker because we always offer jobs and GED and must love and prayer. That day, I took the hand sanitizer and anointed everyone. I put the sanitizer in their hand and say in the name of Jesus and on some, on their heads. If I could feel tense or hurt, I continue to pray with them. So I looked up and the Northside had showed up. I smiled at them to assure them they're welcome.

I was walking by and heard two of the Southside saying bad things about them. So I stood there for a while. I noticed one get on the phone, and in ten minutes, there came two more of them in a few more minutes. There came about five more. In no time, there were at least fifteen of them. All for two guys. I had already announced that if Black lives matter, what are you all here to shout this young man? During the end of two weeks, before we came off in Minnesota, Floyd was murdered by two cops. Supposedly, all Blacks supposed to be angry and more concern about each other.

CHAPTER 20

TESTIMONIES FROM PARENTS

I am a single parent. I have five children ages five to twelve years old. I signed all five into the Hoop Don't Shoot program. I watched the Facebook videos and was impressed with the love shown and the activities that were going on outside, and I wanted my kids to be able to go outside and be safe. I really love reading to them because I never had the time or patience to do that with them. Now they always want me to read to them. My oldest is now playing basketball with the school; Hoop Don't Shoot gave him confidence in himself. I love the program.

—Corintha White

I am a mother trying, at the age of forty-five, to get out of the system. As of today, I take college classes to do better for myself and have more. My youngest is fifteen years old and has been out of school since it started over some gang boys jumping him, so I just put him on vertical so he can still receive his diploma. My two oldest children are in prison. If Hoop Don't Shoot would have been around, I know they could have ended up in the Army instead of prison. This program helped my nineteen-year-old join the Army, and I thank God because I know the young men he was around were gang-affiliated. It also gave me a push to obtain my GED in the college here called DCC.

One day, she was at my house praying and, after praying, informed me to check my house for guns. And to my surprise, I found two guns. "Oh my god," I said in fear. Anything could have happened to me or someone else. I see why it's named Hoop Don't Shoot. Awesome. Thank you, Ms. Angie Dixon.

—Tonya Coles

We always recruit for the military

LAST WORDS

These are wonderful kids performing great tasks. Many of these kids just need a chance and opportunity to show their strengths and smartness. Please consider donating to Hoops Don't Shoot at **angiedixonhds20@qmail.com**.

I also pursued my GED

CPSIA information can be obtained
at www.ICGtesting.com
Printed in the USA
BVHW062203030122
625370BV00021B/1167